TO: ....

FROM: ....

....

DATE:

BroadStreet Publishing Group LLC
Savage, Minnesota USA
Broadstreetpublishing.com

MAJESTIC EXPRESSIONS is an imprint of BroadStreet Publishing Group, LLC.

AMAJESTIC EXPRESSIONS

AMAZING GRACE

© 2021 by BroadStreet Publishing®

978-1-4245-6289-3

Design by Chris Garborg | garborgdesign.com.
Compiled and edited by Michelle Winger.

Printed in China.

21 22 23 24 25 26   7 6 5 4 3 2 1

The birds of the sky
nest by the waters;
they sing among
the branches.

PSALM 104:12 NIV

YOU WILL BE ADORNED WITH BEAUTY AND GRACE!

AND WISDOM'S GLORY WILL WRAP ITSELF AROUND YOU.

MAKING YOU
VICTORIOUS
IN THE RACE

PROVERBS 4:9 TPT

The Lord directs the steps of the godly. He delights in every detail of their lives.

PSALM 37:23 NLT

The law of the
Lord is perfect,
refreshing the soul.

PSALM 19:7 NIV

FLOW WITH HOPE

BY THE POWER OF THE HOLY

SPIRIT

SO THAT YOU MAY OVER

May the God of Hope fill you with all Joy & Peace as you trust in Him

ROMANS 15:13 NIV

The Lord
is all I need.
He takes
care of
me.

PSALM 16:5 NCV

Whom have I in heaven but you?
I desire you more than anything on earth.

PSALM 73:25 NLT

God is able to provide you with every blessing in abundance, so that by always having enough of everything, you may share abundantly in every good work.

2 Corinthians 9:8 NRSV

Because your **love**
is better than **life**, I will praise you.

PSALM 63:3 NCV

From his
innermost
being will
flow rivers of
living water.

JOHN 7:38 NASB

Let the words of my mouth and the meditation of my heart Be acceptable in Your sight, O Lord, my rock and my Redeemer.

PSALM 19:14 NASB

I WILL GIVE THANKS TO YOU, Lord, WITH ALL MY HEART.

PSALM 9:1 NIV

My flesh and my heart may fail, but God is the strength of my heart and my portion forever.

PSALM 73:26 NIV

Even the wilderness and desert will be glad in those days.
The wasteland will rejoice and blossom with spring crocuses.

ISAIAH 35:1 NLT

He will
yet fill your
mouth with laughter
and your lips with
shouts of joy.

JOB 8:21 NIV

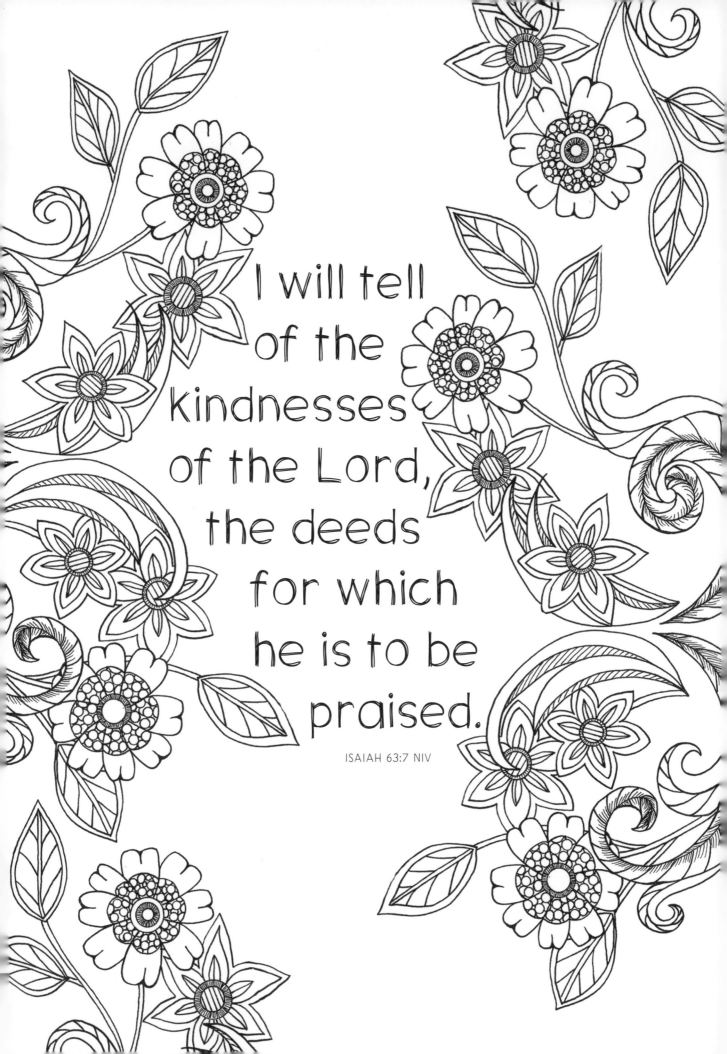

I will tell
of the
kindnesses
of the Lord,
the deeds
for which
he is to be
praised.

ISAIAH 63:7 NIV

Ask and you will receive, and your *joy* will be complete.

JOHN 16:24 NIV

EXODUS 15:2 ESV

Your roots will grow down into God's love and keep you strong.

EPHESIANS 3:17 NLT

The lovers of God
rise up like flowers
in the spring.

PROVERBS 11:28 TPT

IS ANYONE HAPPY? Let him sing songs of Praise.

James 5:13 NIV

THERE IS A
TIME FOR EVERYTHING,
AND EVERYTHING ON EARTH
HAS ITS *special season.*

ECCLESIASTES 3:1 NCV

The eyes
of the LORD
search the
WHOLE EARTH
in order to
STRENGTHEN
those whose
HEARTS
are fully
COMMITTED
to him.

2 Chronicles 16:9 NLT

The fruit of the righteous is a tree of life.

PROVERBS 11:30 NIV

WHATEVER IS
TRUE
WHATEVER IS
HONORABLE
WHATEVER IS
JUST
WHATEVER IS
PURE
WHATEVER IS
LOVELY
WHATEVER IS
COMMENDABLE
IF THERE IS ANY
EXCELLENCE
IF THERE IS ANYTHING
Worthy of
Praise
Think about
these things.

PHILIPPIANS 4:8 ESV

ave given all the green plants as food for every wild animal,
ery bird of the air, and every small crawling animal.

GENESIS 1:30 NCV

From his abundance we have all received one gracious blessing after another.

John 1:16 NLT

Be our strength
every morning;
our salvation
in time of
distress.

ISAIAH 33:2 NIV

The Name
of the Lord
is a
STRONG
TOWER

the
righteous
runs into it
and is safe.

PROVERBS 18:10 NIV

Let my words fall like rain
on tender grass, like
gentle showers on young plants.

DEUTERONOMY 32:2 NLT

Behold, you are BEAUTIFUL, my love!

SONG OF SOLOMON 4:1 ESV

The Grass Withers
the flowers fade

Isaiah 40:8 ESV

BUT THE
WORD
OF OUR GOD
STANDS
FOREVER

Let all the trees of the forest sing for joy.

PSALM 96:12 NIV

THE LORD YOUR GOD IS WITH YOU

He is MIGHTY TO SAVE

He will take great delight in you.

He will QUIET YOU BY HIS LOVE

He will

He will rejoice over you with singing.

Zephaniah 3:17 NIV

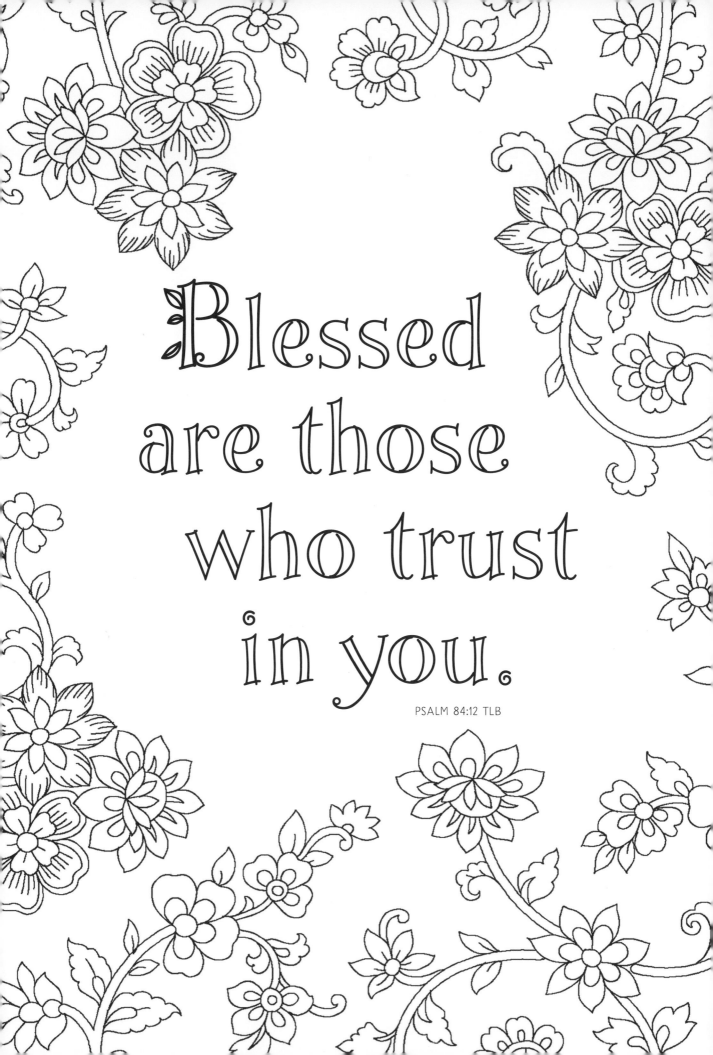

Blessed
are those
who trust
in you.

PSALM 84:12 TLB

Honor and majesty surround him;
strength and joy fill his dwelling.

1 CHRONICLES 16:27 NLT

Your eyes
will see the king
in his beauty and
view a land that
stretches afar.

ISAIAH 33:17 NIV

You should clothe yourselves instead with the beauty that comes from within, the unfading beauty of a gentle and quiet spirit, which is so precious to God.

1 PETER 3:4 NLT

My share in life
has been
pleasant;

my part has
been beautiful.

PSALM 16:6 NCV

LOOK!

I HAVE GIVEN YOU EVERY
SEED-BEARING PLANT
THROUGHOUT THE EARTH AND ALL
THE FRUIT TREES FOR YOUR FOOD.

GENESIS 1:29 NLT

DO NOT GRIEVE FOR THE JOY OF THE LORD IS YOUR STRENGTH

NEHEMIAH 8:10 NIV

You have put joy in my heart,
More than when their grain
and new wine are abundant.

PSALM 4:7 NASB

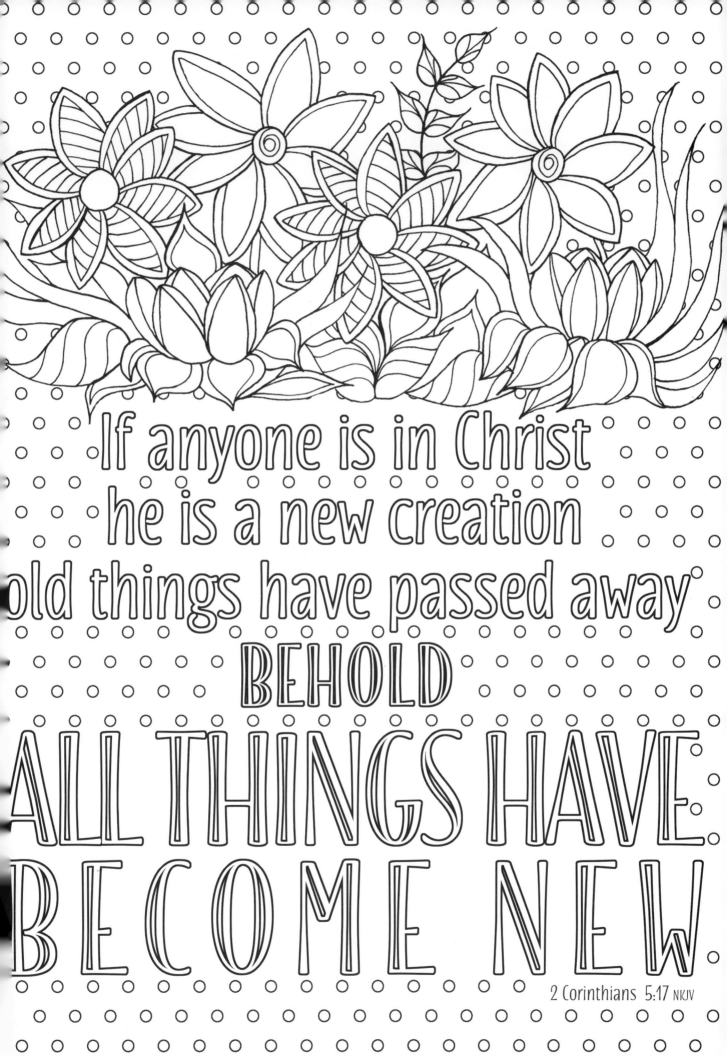

If anyone is in Christ
he is a new creation
old things have passed away
BEHOLD
ALL THINGS HAVE
BECOME NEW

2 Corinthians 5:17 NKJV

My child, listen to your father's teaching and do not forget your mother's advice. Their teaching will be like flowers in your hair or a necklace around your neck.

PROVERBS 1:9 NCV

A CHEERFUL HEART IS GOOD MEDICINE.

PROVERBS 17:22 NIV

You will joyously draw water from the springs of salvation.

ISAIAH 12:3 NASB

Consider the Lilies of the field, how they grow; they neither toil nor spin but I tell you, not even Solomon in all his glory clothed himself like one of these.

Luke 12:27

NASB

Her desert will blossom like Eden,

her barren wilderness like the garden of the Lord.

Joy and gladness will be found there.

ISAIAH 51:3 NLT

YOU WILL SHOW ME THE WAY OF LIFE, GRANTING ME THE JOY OF YOUR PRESENCE AND THE PLEASURES OF LIVING WITH YOU FOREVER.

PSALM 16:11 NLT

For you will go out with Joy
and be led forth with peace

the mountains
and the hills
will break forth
into shouts of
joy before you,
and all the trees
of the field will
clap their hands.

ISAIAH 55:12 NASB

To all who mourn in Israel, he will give a crown of beauty for ashes.

ISAIAH 61:3 NLT

I am the
LIGHT
of the world;
he who follows
Me will not walk
in the darkness
but will have the
Light of life.

John 8:12 NASB

Light is sweet;
how pleasant to
see a new day
dawning.

ECCLESIASTES 11:7 NLT

be truly glad.
there is
wonderful
joy ahead.

1 peter 1:6 nlt

Come to me, all you who are weary and burdened, and I will give you rest.

MATTHEW 11:28 NIV

You will be like a garden that has much water, like a spring that never runs dry.

ISAIAH 58:11 NCV